My Life in a Box

A Life Organizer

LAURIE ECKLUND LONG

Fourth Edition

AGL
PUBLISHING

My Life in a Box…A Life Organizer
Fourth Edition

Published by AGL Publishing
All rights reserved.
P.O. Box 26484 • Fresno, CA 93729 • 559.325.6679.
www.mylifeinabox.com

Note: This book has been written with the understanding that the author
is not engaged in offering legal, accounting, or other professional services. Laws vary from state to state, and readers with specific legal or
financial questions should seek the services of a professional adviser.

Printed in the United States of America

Cover Design: Sarah O'Neal | eve custom artwork
Book Formatting & Design: Sarah O'Neal | eve custom artwork
Portrait of Larry Ecklund by Renée Mason

Dedication

This book is dedicated to the memory of my wonderfully creative dad,
Larry Ecklund, who always encouraged me to be proactive, not reactive.
It is also dedicated to many friends and family who, along with me,
believe that there is value in planning ahead.

Table of Contents

Foreward - Be Prepared

Do you have a family toolbox? I do, but I don't use the tools every day. When I need a hammer, wrench or screwdriver, I know where to find it and how to use it.

When I was young, my grandfather taught me how to use tools. Since he had no male grandchildren, I benefited from his knowledge and learned their proper use.

It was fun. I was taught the difference between a flat head screw driver and a Phillips head screwdriver. I also learned the difference between a hammer and a rubber mallet. For my high school graduation gift, Grandpa gave me a tool box that was loaded with the tools he had previously introduced to me. I still have many of them and use them regularly.

Within the pages of this book I want to help you build a new toolbox. This one is for family emergencies and natural or man-made disasters. As with anything new, it may challenge you. It might even be difficult for you to deal with some of the topics such as personal loss, or writing down your end-of-life wishes. However, I guarantee that if you begin the process, you will be given new tools to successfully deal with major life-experiences you may face in the future.

As with any toolbox, you will probably not use each of the tools right away, but when you need them, they will be there and you will know how to put them to use.

Crisis comes to all of us at some time. It may not always come as a major calamity like a terrorist attack, tornado, hurricane, catastrophic flood or earthquake. More likely it will be a death in the family, an accident, a fire or burglary, but the impact feels much the same.

Several years before 9/11, my personal introduction to crisis management and emergency preparedness occurred when 12 of my family members and friends died over a period of five years. Once the grief and shock wore off, I realized I didn't have the tools to deal with the realities that accompany the death of even one loved one.

I began accumulating all of my first-hand knowledge and assembled a book. Initially it was 135 pages long -- way too much for someone to read in a crisis! So I whittled it down to 32 pages, and The Next 48 Hours became an emergency handbook for over 2,500 individuals, churches, and police and military chaplains. Now, My Life In A Box, A Life Organizer, takes the workbook a step further to help people locate and organize legal, financial and personal documents into one location so that at a moment's notice those documents can be found.

This project took on new urgency in October 2005 when a fire destroyed the homes of two of my friends. Both families were left standing in the street at 4 a.m., with nothing except their pajamas and whatever the fire crews could salvage from their flaming houses. These friends knew about my campaign to be prepared, and after they got resettled, one called me and said, "I have a new chapter for your workbook." She began telling me all of the things she wished she had put into an emergency bag; most important of all, her legal and financial documents, a CD backup of her computer and her medication.

So here I am, on an expanded campaign. The key is KEEP IT SIMPLE, be prepared, get organized and stop procrastinating. I still want the American Dream for my family, but attaining it requires a new mission statement... "Be safe... be wise...be prepared, and keep finding a way to love and embrace life."

Chapter 1

The Price of Procrastination

Pro-cras-ti-nate
Transitive senses: to put off intentionally and habitually.
Intransitive senses: to put off intentionally the doing of
something that should be done.

This definition from the yellowed pages of my Great Grandfather's monstrous old dictionary reads exactly like the definition I found online. Procrastination always means the same thing, and each of us does it in one way or another.

We can laugh about this habit, and some even celebrate it during "National Procrastination Week" (the second week of March). But procrastination comes with a heavy price. When a life crisis occurs, the unprepared person must make decisions amid great stress and pain. Their options are usually fewer, and the likelihood of making unwise decisions much greater. Simple steps of preparedness can save you and your family thousands of dollars and un-needed stress, which is the very reason I wrote this book. It's not a question of if crisis comes, but when.

To put it bluntly, you and each of your family members will encounter a natural disaster, tragedy, terminal illness, or death of a close friend or family member at some time in your life. Our culture in North America doesn't like to face this reality. That's why so few have a plan of action when a loved one dies unexpectedly in a car accident, fire, torna-do, etc. Even when a death due to age or illness happens, the surviving family or friends are often caught without a clue of what to do. Usually shock sets in and everyone runs around looking for insurance policies, obituary infor-mation, end-of-life instructions, and valuables, which are often scattered throughout the house. Ideally, everything should be in one place, and in as few files as possible.

My Life in a Box introduces a simple plan to organize all of your personal, financial, and legal documents and put them in one easy-to-use file that is easy to locate when a crisis arises. In the event of a natural disaster or fire, you can be assured that you will locate all of your documents within five minutes so that you and your family quickly es-cape with everything you need to rebuild your life or relo-cate.

The need for this became abundantly clear to me when a dear friend's mother developed dementia and began hiding valuables throughout her house and garage. My friend found her mother's living trust in the sewing closet, and moved proactively to find other important documents. This "treasure hunt" went on for weeks while my friend began to build files for her mother, using my simple suggestions. Today everything is in order and the files are in a safe and easily accessible place.

The following chapters address a variety of challenges regarding natural and man-made disasters, family emergencies, end-of-life issues, and more. You may not be able to relate to any of these situations right now, but sometime in your life you will.

So don't procrastinate any longer. If you or other family members have not put your personal affairs in order, now is the time to take action. By following the guidelines in this book, you will be able to organize your legal, personal and financial documents and be prepared for anything you may face in the future.

Chapter 2

My Life in a Box

Simplicity is the key to My Life in a Box. By completing these steps, in case of any emergency or disaster you should be able to leave your home within minutes, with everything you need to rebuild your life. It will also help your loved ones easily locate all of your legal, financial, and personal documents if needed.

To begin, locate a box to collect all of your documents, six file folders, a pen, and a portable filing box, all of which may be purchased at your local office supply store.

Create 6 folders. Then use this checklist and locate all of the original documents for every member of the family. Your goal is to put these documents into the six folders. You may decide to keep the folders in one portable file, stored in a heavy duty sealable plastic bag in your Get Away Bag, or in a fire-resistant box or filing cabinet. You may also choose to scan all of your documents and load them onto a password-protected flash-drive. Simply begin the process and then decide how to store these documents in a way that you are comfortable. You may also choose to send a copy to someone.

Emergency Information
☐ Copy and fill out the forms located in the Forms section of the book for yourself and each family member
- My Personal Request
- The Details
- Preferred Contacts

Personal Information:
☐ Birth Certificates
☐ Marriage License
☐ Social Security Cards/ Social Insurance Card (Canada)
☐ Medical & Immunization Records
☐ Copy of Driver's Licenses
☐ Military Papers
☐ Ownership & Registration Papers and License Numbers for Auto, Boat, R.V.

Legal Information:
☐ Will
☐ Living Trust
☐ Durable Power of Attorney Document
☐ Medical Power of Attorney or Health Care Directive
☐ Safe Deposit Box Information, Location, & Key

Insurance Policies:

- ☐ Medical Insurance
- ☐ Long Term Health Care Insurance
- ☐ Life Insurance
- ☐ Burial (Funeral) Insurance
- ☐ Homeowners Insurance
- ☐ Car Insurance

Real Estate:

- ☐ Property Deeds (or location of originals)
- ☐ Current mortgage, rental or lease documents
- ☐ Deed to cemetery plot if previously purchased

Investments:

- ☐ Bank Accounts, Credit Unions
- ☐ Copies of Credit Cards (Front & Back)
- ☐ IRA, 401K (USA) CRA, RRSP (Canada)
- ☐ Stock Certificates
- ☐ Mutual Funds
- ☐ Certificate of Deposits
- ☐ Bonds

Other things to consider:

In your file, keep an extra copy of house and car keys.
Take digital photos of the outside and inside your home to include furniture and other belongings in case your home is destroyed. The digital photos may be scanned into your

computer and saved on a flash (thumb) drive or CD and kept in your file, once again proving what you own.

Once you have collected everything in one box, begin to put each document into one of the six file folders. Throw out old papers and empty envelopes as you go. You may find other important documents not listed on the previous page so figure out what file they best fit into.

Remember, My Life in a Box is a life-organizing tool to help you get started. The simplicity of this system is using six files for everything but don't get frustrated if you have to adapt the files to your own needs.

The Emergency file is just for that purpose. If there is an emergency, those details will be the first ones you and your family will need to access. Ideally you will want to put all of your original documents in the folders and then into a fire resistant box or filing cabinet.

If you have access to a copier, create a second file to put in your Get Away Bag. If you are technologically talented, scan your documents onto your computer and then burn them onto a CD or flash drive, to be kept in your Get Away Bag. You may also send a duplicate file, CD or flash drive to a relative or friend in another town for safekeeping.

No matter what you choose to do with your duplicate file, make sure to tell a member of your family, close friend or attorney about your life organizer and where it is located in case of an emergency. Make sure and write a personal letter to each family member as my grandfather did (Page 57).

Last but not least, each member of the family should copy and fill out the Emergency Personal Inventory Form, (Page 61) which should be taken with you on ANY trip. It is also a vital part of your Get Away Bag (Page 63) so that you are prepared to grab it and run.

The following pages contain information you will need to prepare for a major emergency or the death of a loved one. That includes you! Pre-need planning for your own death is a loving gift you can provide for surviving relatives whether it is your spouse, children, or siblings.

- ***Page 65—Checklist:*** A quick view of what to do, who to call, and how to plan after someone dies.

- ***Page 67—My Personal Request:*** Copy and distribute to each family member. It is a simple way to communicate how you want to be laid to rest. This will inform surviving family members of your wishes so that they don't have to guess their way through the process.

Be specific. Use extra sheets of paper if you have to. It's your last request!

- **Page 69—The Details:** Complete all of the vital information on this form. It is necessary when you fill out the legal forms at the funeral home or crematorium. Again, make copies of the forms for each family member and fill in the blanks. If for some reason you do not have all of the   information; fill the space with "unknown."

- **Page 71—Preferred Contacts:** List important contacts and the location of all legal documents. Make copies of the forms for each family member. Ideally these documents should be kept in a fire resistant box or file, and the contents of your safe deposit box should be listed on paper in the file.

Also remember, if you live in an area that is susceptible to hurricanes, floods, tornados, or earthquakes, you may have a difficult time retrieving the contents of your safe deposit box if the bank is affected by a natural disaster.

Chapter 3

Emergency & Natural Disaster Stories

There are many websites that you may visit to access specific directions on how to survive a natural disaster that may occur in your town. The Red Cross and www.ready.gov provide vital information on the Internet and I visit them often as valuable resources. The following stories represent first hand experiences that I've received from people who have faced and survived unusual challenges during and after emergencies and natural disasters. This first story is from my own family's experience.

Read the Fine Print on Insurance Policies
"Grandma was just in a car accident and I'm on my way to the scene. Call me back in 10 minutes." It was my son calling my cell phone. I was 5,000 miles away from home on vacation.

After an agonizing 10 minutes, I called Josh back. By then he had arrived to find Grandma sitting on the ambulance gurney, looking alert and talking to the EMT. Josh told me if he had seen the two mangled cars first, he would have not believed she was alive. My mother missed a red light and was broadsided by a young woman going 40 miles an hour. Miraculously, only Mom was seriously hurt. She was taken to the hospital where she was diagnosed with a broken pelvis and severe bruising.

My sister stepped into this crisis with amazing focus and perseverance. Because of our previous work, putting all of Mom's legal documents in one location, she was able to quickly access Mom's medical and car insurance policies, call the insurance representative, and get the ball rolling. She worked with doctors, hospital staff, radiologist, police, and even had to hunt down the towing company to find what was left of the car.

Even though we had everything in place, we did not know what each of those policies covered because we never needed to know! Up until this accident, Mom was a healthy 80-year-old woman, living in her own home and enjoying a full life. She was always out and about, helping others in their time of need, including me and my sister who had gone through our own medical crises just six months before her accident.

People spend hundreds of dollars annually on car, health, disability and life insurance, but few of us know the details of our coverage. That's why knowing your insurance agent, and being able to access the toll free number of your insurance company in a hurry is so valuable.

My sister called the toll free number for Mom's car insurance company and got answers quickly. Having good insurance can take much of the stress out of a crisis such as this, but even if you have good insurance, it's wise to read the fine print of your policy before any hospitalization.

When it came to Mom's long-term coverage, we just "assumed" what the policy provided, so we didn't call her agent to get details.

After four days in the hospital and 14 days in the rehabilitation hospital, Mom was released to go home. We were not aware that Mom's long-term health insurance policy "kicked in" only if she had been in a convalescent facility for 15 days. If we would have known those details, we could have made other plans and Mom would have had funding for a home health care nurse. Because of this oversight and because neither my sister nor I could lift or bathe her, we had to go to "Plan B." We contacted an in-home care organization. With their assistance and the help of several friends, Mom recovered and continued living independently in her home.

Through this experience, we learned some tough lessons about insurance plans. We now attach a 3"x 5" card to each insurance policy, listing the benefits and requirements of the policy for quick access in case of another emergency.

17

As you do this, be sure to include the name of the insurance company, policy number, agent's name, local and toll free phone numbers, beneficiary (if there is one) and all of the vital details of the policy. In cases of a home fire, the insurance agencies usually respond immediately. In a natural disaster, the response time can be longer because of the numbers of people filing insurance claims.

You can also call your agent and ask for the details regarding your policy. Calling your agent is a great way to keep in touch and put them to work for you. It is also important to make sure you still have enough coverage, especially in regards to your auto and homeowners insurance.

After Mom's accident, the insurance company took over a month to total the car and send her a check based on its current value. Based on my research, that's an average response time. The hospitals were paid directly and because of the great policies she had in place she had no out-of-pocket expenses. When I had surgery a few months earlier, it took a month to finalize everything related to my insurance payments. My coverage was 70% so each medical service provider (the hospital, five doctors and three labs) allowed me to make payments. Each treated me well as long as I communicated with them and sent a monthly payment.

The Emergency Personal Inventory Form on page 61 is vital to keep handy. It may be kept in your wallet or purse

and may also be given to a relative or friend in a sealed en-
velope. I take a copy of it when I travel. To protect myself
from identity theft, I never write down my passwords or full
account numbers. If I need to contact an insurance agent,
they can locate my account by my name and address.

A Katrina Story – A Case for Having Flood Insurance
As told by Trudy Krahn, a MDS Volunteer

Douglas Hill, a 39-year-old father of two decided to go on
a three-day vacation with his family, including his mother.
He and his son and daughter packed their clothes and left
New Orleans thinking they would only be gone three days.
Doug, who is confined to a wheelchair, never dreamed that
everything he and his family packed would be the only pos-
sessions that they would have left of their life in New Orleans where Doug had been born. The family never imag-
ined that as they were leaving town, Hurricane Katrina was
arriving.

Their trip took them to Texas where they watched with
horror as the news showed only roofs of what had been
their city and their neighborhood. Friends confirmed that
their neighborhood was under water and it would remain
that way for six weeks. Some had family they could turn to
but not so for Doug's family. All of their extended family
had also lost their homes. His mother lost her home and
her car. Doug has been deeded his grandfather's home by

his mother but he would not be back to claim it for another 1 ½ years.

This story however is not without a few miracles. While staying in a Texas hotel, they ran into one of his mother's grandsons. A nephew who, with his five children, rode out the storm for three days in their attic, also showed up at the same hotel.

In spite of the joyful reunion with other family members, their struggles were just beginning. Insurance companies reneged on their policies claiming that it wasn't Katrina that did the damage but the flooding resulting from damaged levies. Doug's mother only received a fraction of what her house was insured for. This, together with dishonest contractors and lost jobs made their return to normal life in New Orleans very difficult.

Doug heard about the Mennonite Disaster Service and miraculously they took on his case. Although images of the flood are still vivid, he now has hope for the future as MDS is totally renovating and remodeling his home and making it wheel chair friendly.

Earthquakes Do Not Happen in Finland
By Taina

It was in my junior year at high school in Finland. It was springtime and we only had a little over a month left of school year. As part of our class assignment we were given several emergency topics to choose from and had to make a class presentation of our chosen topic. Our group chose "Home Storage"- as a topic.

The day of our class presentation arrived. We were so excited about our topic and truly felt that everyone should have at least a two-week supply of food and drinking water. But to our horror, our teacher mocked and ridiculed us openly after our presentation. Not because of our presentation, but the topic, home storage.

"No one needs a two-week supply of food in Finland, we don't have earthquakes or tornados". Her words echoed in my mind repeatedly and soon the class followed our teacher's lead and laughed and mocked us. We hoped the ground would open up and swallow us.

About two weeks later my birthday arrived, April 26, 1986. I went to school as usual. Without warning our school day was interrupted with sirens. The sirens went on and on and we were filled with anxiety, what has happened?

Soon government officials appeared in their emergency vehicles and ordered everyone inside. They told us that there had been an explosion at a nuclear power plant in Russia and it was leaking deadly poison into the air. We were to go home as soon as possible, to close all doors and windows and remain inside. We were to watch TV and wait for further information.

TV channels at school were filled with alarming news. In Russia, the water was polluted, crops and fruits and berries were polluted. All cattle outside during the past 48 hours had to be destroyed.

I held a sleeve to my nose and mouth, hurried home and opened our cupboards. To my relief, we had plenty of supplies because my mother always prepared for emergencies.

The summer passed and my senior year began. I ran into the teacher who had so humiliated me. To my amazement, she stopped me and offered heart-felt apologies for her bad behavior and also for not taking the topic seriously. Chernobyl had taught her and us all a valuable lesson. You never know what happens or when-- be prepared ALWAYS

Ice Storms in Kansas
By Janet Wendland

The weather in Kansas can be brutally extreme, from blizzards and subzero temperatures in winter to severe thunderstorms with damaging winds, hail and flooding in the summer.

People living here are quite pragmatic about those events and are probably more prepared than most to deal with emergency conditions.

It is normal to keep a winter emergency kit in your car, to keep the ice melted and a snow shovel handy. Year-round, most of us have an emergency stock of bottled water, non-perishable foods, candles, lanterns, and battery operated flashlights and radios handy. This said, I don't believe anyone was totally prepared for the devastating ice storm that we experienced in December 2007.

On December 11th, rain started falling mid-afternoon. The temperature was in the 40's and we were glad to get the much-needed rainfall. The rain continued, and by mid-evening freezing rain and temperatures fell into the 20's. The freezing rain accumulated on trees, power lines, streets and sidewalks.

After going to bed, it was eerie to see green sparks and strobe light effects flashing outside as the neighborhood power lines were stretched and arcing. The night sounds were eerie too as I could hear the trees groaning under the weight of the ice and then the snapping of branches. When I awakened, the neighborhood looked like a war zone with full-grown trees toppled and strewn everywhere. Trees and limbs continued to moan, snap and topple during the day. Many trees fell on power lines and caused wide spread power outages. Other falling trees pulled electric boxes off houses and caused numerous house fires. Some power lines, though downed, were still live and caused fire dangers.

I was very fortunate as I only sustained minor damage to the rain gutters on my house from falling limbs and only lost power for about four hours. Many people suffered major loses when limbs fell through roofs, broke windows or fell on vehicles. Much of the town was without power for 4-12 days.

Few individuals own emergency generators and so warming shelters were opened at various locations around town and were soon filled to capacity. Churches took names of people willing to open their homes to neighbors and acted as liaisons in getting people sheltered. Once electricity was restored, people were able to return to their homes, the cleanup began. The food in refrigerators and freezers had spoiled, houseplants had frozen, and some waterlines had burst. Much electrical equipment was 'fried' from the sporadic power surges.

This experience has made me consider how to hone my personal emergency plan and be better prepared. Here are some changes I've made that have given me a new peace of mind:

- I have a working, pot-bellied stove and hired a chimney sweep so I can use it without it being a fire hazard
- I have reread my homeowner's insurance policy, and now know that I should take photos of the food I might discard, as my policy will pay for the replacements.
- I have also purchased a manual can opener for the canned goods I have in stock.

- I've learned how to manually release and open the automatic garage door.
- I've located the main water shutoff valve.

House on Fire
By Sandra Angelo

Most of us who live in residential neighborhoods in San Diego, California were very content with the reality that San Diego is not known for tornados, earthquakes, floods or any of the other notorious disasters. However, my reality changed a few years ago.

I teach people who don't have one lick of talent how to draw. I developed an entire curriculum of books, companion DVD's, magazine columns plus, I had well over 900 pieces of art that I used in my business.

One Sunday morning I woke up and saw that the sky was filled with smoke. I turned the television on and found out that there was a fire in Lakeside, which was 30 miles away. I wasn't very concerned but I did toss a few items in the car. But since I didn't have an organized plan, what I put in the car was very random.

I continued on with my work and then all of a sudden I saw this gorgeous orange sky, so I stepped outside to take pictures of it and heard a siren and a loudspeaker announcing "Evacuate immediately, your life is in danger...get out NOW".

I ran back into my house and grabbed a few pictures off of a dresser and dashed into my car and sped away as fast as I could and joined a long line of cars filled with people who were also evacuating our neighborhood. As I looked in my rear-view mirror, there were big walls of smoke and flames quickly following behind us.

2400 homes were totally destroyed. I went back to my neighborhood to see my home and when I arrived, it looked like a war zone, everything was just ashes. All of my business, including 900 pieces of art sat in the rubble. 17 years of work, was gone.

It took me over three years to rebuild my life. Arduous paperwork, phone calls, reclaiming my identity with a new social security card, driver's license, birth certificate, passport and everything you can possibly think of.

As I surveyed the ashes of what use to be my home and business I knew I would have to totally rebuild every area of my life. I could have saved myself years of agonizing hassles dealing with the government and all kinds of agencies if I had been more prepared. I also should have scanned all my art so that I would at least have jpeg files of the art.

Four years later, almost to the day, another fire hit San Diego burning 1,800 homes. This time I had photocopied all my important papers and sent them to my sister in Arkansas. All of my new art has been scanned and I have sub-masters of my DVD's in Orange County. I am better prepared!

Chapter 4

Children & Emergency Preparedness

Babies & Toddlers

When you are building your emergency plan, make sure and pack a Get Away Bag for your little ones. Clothing, toys, extra baby bottles, snacks, baby wipes, zip-lock bags, and diapers, diapers, diapers! Can you imagine having to leave your home in five minutes and forgetting the diapers?

If you have a car seat and stroller, attach an emergency card to each of them. The emergency card should have the child's name, your name, address, and cell number for both parents, or a parent and another family member. Why? In case of an accident, and if the adult is not able to talk, how will the authorities know who the children are and who to contact? Did I do this when I was a young mother? NO! I didn't think about it because I was invincible. Nothing was going to happen to me. Back then, I didn't even have a cell phone.

School Age Children

As you are building your Get Away Bags, be sure to include your children in the process. Don't do everything for them or they will not take ownership when there is an emergency. Make sure to have crayons, markers, coloring books, and other non-electronic activities in their bag. When the power goes off and batteries are not available, simple activities will be appreciated.

Check with your children's school and ask for an approved copy of the emergency plan. In case of a fire, or natural disaster, will they keep the children at school for you to pick up, or will they send them home?

Without creating fear, spend some time talking with your children about your own family emergency plan. If parents are at work when there is a natural disaster or fire, where will you meet? How will you communicate? Find a way to communicate within your family now, so that if the situation arises, you will know the schools emergency plan and how you and your children will respond.

Teens

Having grown up in the 1950's with air raid sirens going off each month, I think I went a little overboard once or twice as I tried to prepare my children for potential dangers. However, one conversation was quite effective. That conversation happened when my son was 14 and he had an opportunity to go to San Francisco with his dad and grandfather to see a baseball game.

I had never talked with him about what to do in case of an emergency if he was away from home. I explained to him that he needed to be aware that emergencies happen when we least expect them and that he must learn how to think his way through it and not give into fear. Fear is a natural reaction, but never let fear keep you from thinking clearly, getting help and getting home.

What I told him did not alarm him because he already knew that San Francisco was known for earthquakes since his great-great-grandparents lost everything in the 1906 earthquake.

During that 15 minute conversation I mentioned that in case of a car accident, earthquake, fire, or any other type of incident, if he could walk, talk and use his brain, he could get home safely. I explained that some day he might face a situation where his dad and I were not around and as long as he was not injured, he could use his brain to think and his feet to walk or run for help and get to a safe place.

My son is now an adult with his own family but if you bring up that "talk" he still remembers what happened, and is amazed at the timing of that conversation. He went on the trip to Candlestick Park with his dad and grandfather. They had a great time and there were no concerns for his safety at all. In fact he came running into the house and immediately told me that I really had nothing to worry about.

However, that following week he and I were watching the World Series on TV and all of a sudden the screen went dark. When the television station finally came back on the reporter explained that there was just an earthquake in San Francisco. My son looked at me and said "Mom, how'd you know that was going to happen"? I just told him that mothers have a direct line to God and to this day I hope he still believes that is true! (smile)

The conversation that I had with Josh before he went to the Giant's game, and the one that I had later with his sister, were vital conversations that I believe teach our children how to use their brains, use their feet, and find a way to survive.

Chapter 5

Photo Archiving & In-Home Survival

Photos are a valuable part of life not only as part of our history, but also as a way to build wonderful memories of current and future events.

What a tragedy to lose everything in a home fire or natural disaster. As my friend Sandra Angelo noted, when she was told that she had to leave her home because of a fire, she only took a few pictures from her dresser. What if she had been able to archive all of her artwork and photos?

In case of a disaster, there will be a limit to how many albums you can carry from your home. Now, through the wonders of technology, we are able to scan and archive photos on free (or inexpensive) Internet sites. Photos may also be scanned onto a flash drive (thumb drive) or CD and then put it in your Emergency File or Getaway Bag. If you do not use a computer, you can create one photo album of your favorite photos and store it in a plastic bag and put it in your Get Away Bag.

I enjoy taking pictures and started looking into storing my digital images on the Internet in 2006. In a search engine, I typed the words *free online photo storage* and was stunned at the variety of free ways to store my photos. Today I have 40 photo albums stored and I am able to share those photos with family and friends. Each time I take a trip, visit family or friends, or take care of my grand-children, I take pictures with my digital camera, and load them into one of my on line photo albums where they are ready to share.

If you have a large collection of printed photos, make time and scan them onto your computer. Once they are in a computer file you can easily transfer them into an on line source. If you do not have a scanner, ask a family member or friend for help, or pay to have special photos scanned into jpg images and stored on a CD, and then transfer them into your on line account.

If you have no idea what I am writing about, just get on the Internet, go to a search engine, type in the words *free online photo storage* and see how it works! Once you try this, you will be amazed at how easy the process is and how fun it is to send photos to friends and family. As with any type of technology, please make sure to keep a backup copy on a CD or flash drive just in case the online business crashes, sells, or changes their membership policy.

In-Home Survival

The Red Cross recommends a 72 hour in-home survival kit and I encourage you to visit their website for a complete survival plan. However, most of the people I meet in my travels and workshops do not have anything in place if they had to stay home during a disaster. This is a vital component of your emergency toolbox.

Another argument I hear relates to the family budget. This is why I have assembled a very simple list of items that will help you begin to purchase and start building in-home survival supplies. The list covers basic food, water, tools, and first aid items for your family and it is spread over 4-months. By the time you complete the list, you will have a great start. The list is printed on pages 78 through 81.

As you begin to collect items, take time and think about how you will pack and store them. Items such as food and first aid supplies should be packed on top. Also make sure that the containers are not too heavy so that you can quickly move them outside in case of a house fire or other emergencies. Large plastic storage drums with airtight and watertight lids or rectangle stackable plastic containers with wheels work great.

Chapter 6

Personal Loss...
What We Don't Learn in School

Taken from the book "The Next 48 Hours"

The next 24 pages cover the topic of end-of-life issues and supply valuable tools for your emergency tool box. Personal loss is a subject that we have a tendency to ignore until we face the death of a loved one or we, ourselves are terminal. At that point we are in shock and dealing with grief and we can make very costly decisions. By following a few simple suggestions in the next few pages, you can lessen the stress for yourself and your family as you go through the process.

I have spent over a decade helping people prepare for this aspect of life and within the next few pages is vital information that you may someday need. Here's my story and what my family and I learned.

I enjoyed going to weddings when I was young. I loved the music, the flowers, the party, the food and the gifts for the young couple. The entire experience was magical. Then I got married and saw a different side of the experience. It was work. Weddings can take months to organize and are a major expense...but what a day!

A similar amount of emotional intensity, organizing, and spending was required of us during the week of June 16, 1997. On that day, without warning, my father died. Dozens of decisions relating to his death had to be made, and most took place in just 48 hours.

Few of us are ever fully prepared for the loss of a close family member, but a sudden and unexpected death hits even harder. Just the day before, our family was honoring Dad on Father's Day. He loved having the family together, so we went to lunch at a Chinese restaurant. We ate lots of food, laughed, and Dad and Mom talked about their trip to visit friends and relatives in Los Angeles the next day.

They had just finished packing when Dad began to experience indigestion and shortness of breath. Within 30 minutes he was in the hands of paramedics who administered CPR. They transported him to a nearby hospital where he passed away.

After we left the hospital, I took Mom to her home and stayed with her. We got little, if any sleep. The next morning we were both up by 6:00. We were numb, but knew that we needed to face reality, and begin planning Dad's funeral and memorial service. It was going to be a huge celebration of Dad's life, just like a wedding, but it all had to be planned within 48 hours. Thankfully Dad had pre-planned arrangements, and we had lots of friends to help.

What we did not realize was the staggering financial and emotional cost of a family member's death. Forty-eight hours is the average time it takes to prepare for most funerals. During those 48 hours your body goes into shock. It is hard to make decisions in that state. That's why preparing for this part of life is so necessary.

It is important to understand that the funeral industry is run by business people who provide services. These services are not free, and the more complicated the arrangements, the more costly the services. A funeral or memorial service requires coordination between several businesses and organizations. If a typical funeral is chosen you will need to:

1. Locate a funeral home or cremation service.
2. Order a casket or cremation container.
3. Purchase a grave and find out when it can be prepared (Saturday or Sunday may require overtime fees.)
4. Order a casket spray and family flower arrangements.
5. Choose an alternative remembrance for friends and acquaintances such as a memorial gift to a church or organization.
6. Write an obituary and find a picture for the obituary and memorial service folder (if you choose to have one).
7. Plan the service, music, and food.
8. Contact family and friends.
9. Figure out the cost of all of the above and how to pay for it.

Our experience with Dad's passing may not be anything like your experience. However, after talking with others who have come through this difficult time, we all agree that we were not prepared for this inevitable experience called death.

Three years prior to Dad's passing, my grandfather had a major stroke. The doctors expected him to die within a couple of days. Mom and Dad recently had helped a couple in our church with unexpected funeral plans. They were impressed with a local funeral director and how he presented his services with no pressure. We realized the need to make immediate funeral plans for Grandpa.

A representative from the funeral home came to my parent's home and we sat around the kitchen table where he presented information regarding burial costs, caskets, pre-need insurance, and obituary information. It was the most uncomfortable feeling I've ever experienced. By the end of the meeting, we had picked out Grandpa's casket, planned his funeral, and paid for his pre-need insurance.

Then Dad turned to Mom and said, "This isn't fun, but it is necessary. Let's just fill out these forms for both of us and get it out of the way." Within 30 minutes they duplicated Grandpa's plans, legal information, and family details. Mom and Dad's pre-need folder and insurance were complete. The projected cost for the modest service they planned totaled $4,000 each. It covered the funeral home services, casket, and cemetery services.

The next day Dad went to a local cemetery and purchased six plots. I asked him why six, and he said that he
got a great deal on them.   We both chuckled and yet little
did we know that Grandpa would recover from the stroke
and outlive Dad. We ended up using one of those cemetery
plots and pre-need plans for Dad before using the plans we
had prepared for Grandpa.

Most funeral homes offer some kind of pre-need insurance plan. However, some plans may not be transferred if
you move out of the area or plan a burial outside your own
region. Other ways to pre-plan for these expenses include:
putting money into a special savings account, taking out a
Certificate of Deposit, or purchasing a term life insurance
policy for each family member. Most funeral homes and
cemeteries will expect payment in full at the time the arrangements are made.

In pre-planning, contact several funeral homes and cemeteries by phone to compare their prices. Make copies of
the forms on pages 73 and 76 and interview funeral homes
and cemeteries regarding their fees. We want the "best"
for our loved one, yet costs can quickly add up. Also, you
are not required to purchase everything that the funeral
home offers. You may build your own casket or purchase
one from a variety of companies on the Internet that can be
quickly delivered to the funeral home, saving you several

hundred dollars. You may even find a cemetery plot for sale in the newspaper, as my in-laws were able to do. They found two cemetery plots in a small town near their home.

They purchased both plots for less than half of the original cost of one plot.

If you are faced with a sudden death, copy the forms on pages 73 and 76. Have friends call several funeral homes and cemeteries and fill in the information on the cost of their services. It is not necessary to fill in all of the blanks. Simply request and compare the basic fees and embalming costs.

Have a family meeting and choose a funeral home and cemetery based on your findings. If your loved one has been taken to a funeral home that you decide not to use, you have the legal right to transfer your loved one to another funeral home. You must know your options. Making emotional decisions can cost you a fortune.

Current funeral prices are listed at www.mylifeinabox.com/funeral.pdf

Chapter 7
Funerals & Other Important Details

When a Death Occurs

If your loved one is terminally ill, select a funeral home immediately.

After his or her death, the hospital or nursing home will want to know your plans immediately. If your loved one dies before you have selected a funeral home, don't be pressured into a hasty decision on where to take the body. If the hospital or nursing home recommends a funeral home and makes the pick-up arrangements for you, once again, you may choose to move your loved one to another funeral home that is more compatible with your family needs. You are not locked into your first choice.

Death at Home

If your loved one dies at home, first call the doctor since he or she can provide the cause of death for local authorities and sign the death certificate. This is especially important if your loved one has a terminal illness or has recently been ill. Second, contact the funeral home or crematorium for pick up. If the family doctor or doctor-on-call is not available, and the death is unexpectedly sudden, call your local coroner or medical examiner for specific directions. They may ask you to call 911 and inform the operator of the death. At that point, the 911 operator will send the proper authorities. If your city has a fee for 911 service calls, the coroner or medical examiners office should have another option. Usually the fire department or an ambulance will arrive first to verify the death.

The police department will send an officer to fill out the legal forms and call the coroner's office for pick up if there is no known cause of death. This process may take several hours, and your family may use this time to gather at home for prayer and to begin making plans.

When my Aunt Ginny died at home, we called 911. It took 10 minutes for the ambulance, 25 minutes for the police, and two more hours for the coroner's van to arrive. If the family doctor is available to pronounce the death, the body may be taken directly to the funeral home of your choice. Once they are contacted for pickup, it may take 20 minutes to four hours. If the person is in a hospital or nursing home, the facility will take care of the pronouncement. If the family doctor is out of town, ask the doctor-on-call to read the file and sign the death certificate; otherwise, the body might go to coroner's office for an autopsy.

Out of Town Deaths

Contact the local police. They will know the protocol. Ideally you should contact the funeral home in your town, and they will help arrange to have your loved one returned home. If the death occurs away from home, you will be required to have your loved one embalmed before he or she is returned home.

Before taking a trip all family members should copy, fill out and pack the form located on page 49, The Details. If a loved one dies while out of your home country, it may take several days or weeks to have the death certificate signed and the body released so the information on this form is vital. The local authorities should help you with your plans, and your home country's embassy can help you deal with the legalities. If your loved one is traveling alone in another country and dies, you may have complications. If you can't get the help you need, call your local government representatives and put them to work. They were elected to serve the public so don't think twice about asking for their help. They have access to services that will get your loved one home! Also check with the airlines regarding special discounted Bereavement Fares.

Before Planning a Burial

Make sure the cemetery plot is purchased and the cemetery gives you their available times since they have to open and close the grave. What a shock to make your entire funeral plans and then find out the cemetery closes at noon on Saturday and is not open on Sundays. Those that are open may add overtime charges for weekend and holiday funerals.

Obituary Information

Within 11 months, my mother, sister and I wrote obituaries for three family members. We wanted to say so much about each person but we had limited space, limited time and were still functioning in a state of shock. We were stunned when we received the bill for my father's obituary. It was over $400 for a small 2½" x 5" obituary with a photo.

As part of your planning, look through your local newspaper and read a few obituaries. Create a mock obituary, call the newspaper, and ask for a quote. This will provide you with a good standard as you prepare obituaries in the future. Most obituaries are charged by the line, with an additional charge for a photo.

Before you call the newspaper about placing an obituary, check with your local funeral home. They may include the cost of the obituary in their service fee.

If you include a photo, make sure it is clear and has good contrasting colors. Otherwise the photo in the newspaper will appear light and possibly fuzzy. If you have several photos available, take them to the newspaper, or send them a digital copy by email and ask them to pick the one that will print the best.

Choosing a Grave Marker

Before you purchase a grave marker from the funeral home, take some time and look at your options. You do not need to make a final decision on a marker before the funeral. Contact a local monument company and find out what they have to offer.

If your loved one was in the military, the cemetery or funeral home can order a free bronze military marker. It will have the name, dates of birth and death, and their branch of military service.

How Many Original Death Certificates Will Be Needed?

One of the responsibilities of a funeral home or crematorium is to file the notice of death with the city or county where the death occurs. In turn, they will ask how many original copies of the death certificate you will need. The cost of each original certificate may vary from $5 to $20. The responsible party paying the bills may need original death certificates for many of the following items:

- Life Insurance Benefits
- Union Death Benefits
- Social Security Death Benefits
- Veterans Administration Death Benefits
- Home, car, health insurance changes
- Bank, investment, real estate, & auto transfer title changes
- Extra Requests (some organizations may accept photocopies.)

What About Flowers?

In some cultures, the family traditionally orders a floral casket spray; however, it is just as appropriate to drape the
casket with a flag, a family quilt, or a homemade flower arrangement. One friend picked roses from his garden and
gave them to the guests at a graveside service. At the end
of the service, each guest placed the rose on the casket as
they left.

Flowers should be part of your pre-need arrangements
so that you understand your options. Make calls to several florists and ask them what they offer in a floral stand-
up spray or casket spray for $75. You'll find out quickly if
they are willing to work with you. One local florist said she
could use lots of greenery and two-dozen assorted flowers
for $75. If you have a larger budget, ask what they can offer
within your price range.

Some florists actually specialize in funerals, and we found
one that had many wonderful suggestions for the funerals
of my father and grandfather. They can also help in more
difficult circumstances. For example, my mother-in-law's
funeral was out of town, and we volunteered to locate a
floral spray for the casket. Since her service was graveside
and we needed to travel two hours to reach the cemetery,
we were concerned how well the flowers would survive in
the May heat. In the end, we were thrilled to find a florist who rented a beautiful silk flower casket arrangement

for $45. It held up beautifully, and we returned it the following day.

For Grandpa's winter graveside service we had an arrangement of cedar boughs with baby's breath and white roses. Grandpa loved the mountains and yet was a gentleman so the arrangement was perfect.

While it's wonderful to have flowers at the funeral or memorial service, families often wonder what to do with them afterward. It's entirely appropriate to share them with family members, your church, or a local nursing home. You may also want to dry a few flowers for a lasting arrangement.

Photo Displays

Photos are a great way to share memories at a funeral or memorial service. At Dad's memorial service, we located a special photo that we had enlarged to 11" X 17" and framed. We also found six negatives of Dad with the grandkids and other family members. The same photo shop made 8"x10" prints from the negatives and we placed those framed family pictures in the entrance of the church for people to view as they arrived at the service. The 11"x17" print was put on an easel by the altar. If negatives are not available, photos can be easily scanned and enlarged on a computer and emailed to a photo shop for printing.

At my grandfather's graveside service, a framed 5"x 7" photo was placed on the casket. Since it was a closed-casket funeral, it helped each of us to see his picture during the service. My aunt chose to be cremated and not have a service, so we decided to display photos at a memorial luncheon in her home. We located a variety of photos that represented her creative life, sorted them and taped them together so they would fit into 8"x10" frames. Before framing them, I made color copies for family members. The originals were framed and shown along with older framed black and white photos. Altogether we created 10 displays for people to view during the luncheon.

There is a lot to be said about a video collage of your loved one's life. It's a wonderful addition to the funeral or memorial service if a friend or family member has time to create it. Many times the funeral home is able to provide this service for a fee.

Chapter 8

More Stories & Lingering Issues

A Seagull Story

One challenge in planning my father's funeral occurred when we found out his choice of casket style was not in stock. It never occurred to me that there was a casket warehouse that could run out of caskets! But it happened, and we chose another style within our price range. It was a lovely metallic blue-gray with eagles painted in enamel on each exterior corner.

Dad loved the scripture in Isaiah 40:31 "They that wait on the Lord shall renew their strength. They will mount up with wings like eagles..." (KJV)

At the viewing, the night before Dad's service, my then, 11-year-old niece came up to me and said, "Aunt Laurie, those aren't eagles on Grandpa's casket... those are seagulls." I quickly said, "No Melody, those are eagles." She was very persistent and said "Aunt Laurie, those are seagulls." Knowing we needed to change the direction of the discussion, I looked into her big brown eyes and said, "Melody, today those are eagles." She smiled and said, "And lovely eagles they are!" Those around us saw the humor in the situation, and we laughed as we talked about how beautiful the "eagles" were, and how Dad would have enjoyed the conversation.

Going Through Grief

Grief and shock affects the body like a severe sickness, so don't be alarmed if you periodically feel disoriented. It's also not uncommon to lose your appetite. One valuable bit of counsel that helped us greatly during our times of loss was the importance of eating four to six small meals a day and drinking lots of water. Your doctor may need to prescribe a mild sleeping pill because of insomnia. Allow people to run errands for you and make phone calls to relatives and friends. If you lose a spouse, find a friend or family member to spend a few nights at your house to help you emotionally and physically as you begin to work through the shock. Write down phone numbers of your physician and close family in case you physically crash.

Get Help!

If you are preparing this information for your family before you die, it would be wise to establish a Health Care Directive and Durable Power of Attorney for Health Care. It would also be wise to assign one of your (trustworthy) siblings, children or adult grandchildren as a co-signer on your checking account, savings account, and safe deposit box. If you are injured, hospitalized, or lose your ability to care for yourself, someone will become responsible for your care (and debts).

If you have funds available, a family member can pay your bills if they are on your bank signature card. You may choose to have someone on your checking account, or both checking and savings accounts.

Health Care Directive

If you have been admitted to a hospital for surgery or treatment, you have probably been asked if you have a Health Care Directive. Most surgeries will not take place unless this form is on file.

A Health Care Directive allows you to specify your wishes regarding your health care and whom you choose to make health care decisions for you if you are unable to speak for yourself. The person you choose may be a family member or non-family member. Either way, that person will be your agent and will speak for you. In normal situations you do not need an attorney to make it legal. It usually requires two witness signatures, or the signature of a notary public. Forms may be picked up from your physician, a hospital, an attorney, office supply stores, or on the Internet.

Wills & Trusts

A person who dies without a will or trust may leave a legacy of trouble for his or her family. If you haven't expressed your wishes regarding your estate, the government will decide for you. In several states, even if you have a will, it may take up to two years of costly probate hearings and legal fees before the book is closed on your life.

I once heard a story that challenged me to start looking into setting up a family trust. A business acquaintance that was involved with his brother in a small pet store partnership died from a heart attack. He was only 40 years old and had a wife and two children. He had a simple will, but because of the business, the probate process got complicated. When all was settled, his wife and brother had to sell the business and their homes to pay for the taxes and unexpected expenses involving the partnership.

At the time our family was involved in a business with two unrelated families. I had a long talk with my parents about putting together a Living Trust. They contacted a lawyer and put it in place. At the time of Dad's death, everything was transferred into my mother's name. There were no probate hearings and no taxes to pay. Depending on the size of your estate and the laws in your state, a Living Trust can be a huge savings for your family.

Property Distribution

Several friends have shared how their parents worked out the distribution of their belongings before they passed away. One couple purchased a ledger book and listed all of their belongings, i.e., furniture, appliances, paintings, tools, jewelry, etc. They had the ledger copied and gave copies to each of their children and grandchildren.

In the privacy of their own homes, the children and grandchildren ranked the items from 0-5 with a very strong interest being "5" and "0" showing no interest. The ledger copies were signed by the family members and returned to the parents. This allowed the parents enough time to include the distribution of their belongings in their will. At Christmas, they gave some of their belongings to their children and grandchildren as Christmas gifts. This gave the parents the extra blessing of seeing the family members' responses to their gifts.

Another family received photos of their favorite items in a Christmas card. That way the grandparents would continue to enjoy the furniture or trinkets, but the children and grandchildren knew that when the time came, those items would be theirs and they had the picture as proof!

Sadly, many families experience greed and selfishness when it comes to property distribution after the passing of a family member. Take time. Talk, and don't allow a desire for material things divide your family. Usually, by law, no one is allowed to have access to anything until the will is read and the executor has been put in place. However, make sure someone empties the refrigerator and all trash-cans before the house is locked up.

Face the Grief and Walk Through It

I remember the day my Mom asked us to come over and go through Dad's clothing. It had been four months since his death, and she needed some help with the task. We separated the shirts and slacks into sizes, colors, and styles and put them in another bedroom for distribution. I did just fine until I found a pair of navy twill slacks that Dad wore with his golf sweaters whenever we would go to lunch and discuss the family business. I immediately saw him in my mind's eye, walking up the path to my office, and saying, "Hey kiddo, you ready for lunch?"

I fell apart and cried. Mom came in, looked at the same slacks, and also began to cry! It hurts to have those uninvited memories jump into your mind, but talking about shared memories can speed the healing process.

Most of all don't get "stuck." Face the emotions, walk through the pain you are feeling, talk about the memory with people around you, and then keep going! In the years since then, my family has had occasional tears, but we've had an equal number of laughs as we recounted wonderful memories of Dad.

A First Experience for a Child

When your children experience their first family loss, it's vital to prepare them for what they may experience at the funeral home, service, and cemetery. Alyssa was 10 and Josh was 11½ when our first close family member (Grandpa Long) passed away. We took the children to the family home the day before the funeral and while we were driving, we discussed what they might see at the service and let them ask lots of questions.

Alyssa insisted she needed to see Grandpa Long. We hadn't planned on going to the funeral home. We agreed to take her just before the graveside service. At the last minute Grandma Long also went with us, and it ended up being a special family memory. Grandpa chose his own casket, clothing, and flowers in his pre-need arrangements. He was dressed in his favorite red polyester sports shirt, with a pink carnation on the lapel. He was color blind, but he had his last say on how he wanted to be put to rest. That experience of seeing him one last time gave Alyssa closure.

A friend had a similar experience with her 8-year-old son after the boy's grandfather died. The family planned a cremation and didn't realize their son needed to say his good-byes. Thankfully, the funeral home was able to prepare the grandfather for viewing and the family came to pay their last respects. Grandpa was nicely dressed and covered with a quilt as though he were sleeping. The grandson was able to deal with his grandpa's death, and left a small stuffed toy for Grandpa to take to heaven. Many funeral homes will work with families even when cremation is chosen since cremations often do not occur until five to seven days after the death occurs. There is a fee involved in the viewing preparation, but sometimes it's necessary to have that option.

Children need to understand death as a part of life. Our biggest success after losing so many important people in such a short time, was allowing the children to choose what part of the funeral experience they wanted to participate in. Communication and good family time through these experiences helped them individually deal with the losses. We also turned to professional counselors after our son had experienced the deaths of seven friends and family members within a period of 13 months. It was well worth the expense to hire a professional to help Josh work through those painful experiences.

When Dad died, our daughter wanted us all to be together during those 48 hours after his death. She didn't want to be in school; she didn't want to be home; and she didn't want to be with friends. She said it was better to be doing nothing with family at Grandma and Grandpa's house than to be anywhere else.

Write a Letter

When I was 24, my grandfather died. My mother sent me a copy of a note that was with his will. It was handwritten and it said:

> *"Dear Family.*
> *The last few months have made me realize more than ever that the future is very uncertain and if things don't pan out, this note is to convey all of my love to you individually and collectively. Mom and I have been very happy with all of you.*
> *Love, Dad."*

Those few words on a piece of notepaper touched the lives of my mother and aunt deeply. Grandpa was a man of few words, and praise was not a part of his daily life. For my own family those few words were comforting, healing, and affirming. Take time to write a note to each member of your family or write a corporate letter that can be kept by an attorney or in your pre-need file. Once you're gone, it will be a blessing for your family to read whenever they need to be encouraged.

In Closing

The details and stories found in this book were assembled after a great deal of personal loss. However, after 9/11 and

Hurricane Katrina I realized that any type of loss can devastate a family especially if they are unprepared. Most of the people who were taken out of New Orleans had no way to prove who they were or what they owned. For my family, our faith in God, and our extended family and friends were a great source that we depended on when we faced each loss.

As we prepare for the future, we should be ready to respond and serve each other and our community during emergencies and disasters. I'd like to encourage you to take a Red Cross class and join a local volunteer disaster response organization related to your house of worship or your community. You can find local emergency organizations on the Internet by doing a search for Emergency Preparedness Class (your town), and by visiting the websites of the Red Cross, Homeland Security, and CERT to name a few.

I hope the information in this book will be a positive motivation, and that it will take some of the insecurity and mystery out of facing emergencies.

Natural disasters, fires, car accidents, illnesses, and even death are unfortunately a part of life. There are many facts, figures, and details that each of us would rather ignore. However, if you will make the time to get organized and put YOUR life in a box, when challenges arise, you will be able to face them intelligently and with much support and inner peace.

Forms

As a member of the
My Life in a Box Community,
Get FREE access to many of the
following forms in an electronic format.
For access to the PDF forms and for
future updates please visit

www.mylifeinabox.com/bookowners.html

The forms provided on the following pages maybe duplicated for use with your immediate family members.

Emergency Personal Inventory

If you need to leave your home quickly because of a house fire or natural disaster, or if you are traveling and you need to access personal information, you will want to have the details listed on this form. Once it is filled out, it should be updated regularly and kept in your Get Away Bag. As you begin to build your Get Away Bag, you will find other items to add. This is just a starting point. It's also valuable to keep a copy of this form with you when you travel in case you need to access your various accounts. Each member of your household should have a copy of this form filled out and in their own Get Away Bag.

Medication:

When you have a few pills left from a prescription you take regularly, reorder your new supply and put the bottle with the original label and a four-day supply in your Get Away Bag. That way when you leave your home you will have an original prescription bottle and a few pills. On the back of this form list all of your medications along with the prescription number, prescribing doctor and phone number of the pharmacy.

Credit Card List:

Name of Card | Toll Free # | Account Number (Last 4 digits)

1: _____

2: _____

3: _____

4: _____

Driver's License Number _____

Auto License Number(s) _____

Homeowner's or Renter's Insurance Company

_____

Policy # _____ Toll Free # _____

Car Insurance Company _____

Policy # _____ Toll Free #_____

Bank _____

Account # (last 4 digits)_____

For Computer Users

If you use online banking, account numbers and passwords are vital. If you are relocated somewhere other than your home, you may not have access to this information from your personal computer. Use the back of this form to list your accounts and passwords in a code that you will remember. Also, copy your important computer files onto a CD, or a password-protected USB flash drive. Put the CD or flash drive in your Get Away Bag, and keep a second one in your Emergency File. Plan to update this form at least every three months on the same date you update the clothing in your Get Away Bag. Consider sending a copy of this form and your backup file to a family member or friend in another state.

Cell Phones

During a natural disaster, cell phone companies may not be in service. Make a decision with your family to have one out-of-state/province person for everyone to contact. Make sure everyone has that phone number. As soon as possible, call or text your contact and make sure they know where you are and how you are so that they can let other family members know when they call in. Often a text message will get through when your cell phone call won't.

Family Contact Person: _____

Phone Number _____

How to Plan Your Get Away Bag

Everyone needs what I call a Get Away Bag. This is not a long-term emergency survival bag but one that will get you through 2-3 days. You will need to check with other organizations such as the Red Cross to plan for long-term emergency survival. Once you get started packing this bag, you will find additional things you and your family will need. If you have children, please don't scare them into preparing their bag. Make it fun and have each family member put their bag under their beds or in a closet for easy access and safekeeping. Then, once you have your bag packed, try living out of it for a weekend to see if you have everything you need.

Children and elderly family members should have a bag or backpack with wheels so that it is easy to remove from the house. Mine is a very old carry-on bag with wheels. Each family member should be responsible for his or her own bag. If it is not financially feasible to have a rolling bag, take a pillowcase and allow each child to color it with permanent marker, making sure that its name is on it. After it is decorated, they can pack it and tie off the end with a colored rope or old belt. Their involvement will help them carry some responsibility during an emergency. Also encourage them to pack a small toy or game and make sure to at least pack a deck of cards in your bag!

Don't forget to write a reminder on your family calendar every three months to update the clothing in your bag. You don't want to find winter clothes during the summer!

Clothing
Seasonal clothing that you will update every three months. Sturdy shoes (tennis), 2 pairs of socks, 2-3 pairs of underwear, long pants, shirt, jacket, gloves, hat. This list will change in the summer and the list can include a pair of sandals but you should always have some type of hat to protect yourself from the sun and walking shoes.

Toiletries & Personal Items (Purchase and pack "Travel Size" items if you can)
Toothbrush, toothpaste, deodorant, shampoo and conditioner, soap

in a re-closable plastic bag, mouthwash, 8-10 assorted band aids in a plastic bag, antibacterial cream, 3-4 rubber bands, tweezers, small scissors, hair brush, comb, small bag of makeup (that's the woman in me!!!), chap stick, mirror, medication (a four-day supply of each prescription in the original bottle), cough drops, vitamins, eye drops, bottle of your favorite pain medication like aspirin, female supplies, packet of antibacterial wipes to use as a wash cloth, an empty plastic bag for wet or dirty clothing, flash light & extra batteries, a small travel sewing kit, safety pins, ear plugs, small roll of toilet paper, tissue packet, eye glasses and contacts, address book with email addresses and phone numbers of family contacts.

Odds & ends that one family member can be responsible for:
Pocketknife, matches, extra car key, small can opener, multi-head screwdriver, and small wrench. Small radio (with extra batteries or the crank kind), notepad and pen, small roll of duct tape. Create a CD or a password-protected USB flash drive backup of family computer files, and as much money in small denominations that you can put away and not be tempted to use. Also pack your "My Life in a Box" backup file in your bag using a CD or USB flash drive.

Food & Water:
Because water may leak, several cases of bottled water in a stored for easy access. I keep one case in my car and use it. When my supply gets low, I replace it with other waster bottles in my garage. That way I always have a fresh supply of water on hand.
I have pre-sealed cereal bars and protein bars and almonds in my bag. Help children, elderly parents and pets create a bag specifically for their food and care.

Pets
There are great websites with emergency preparedness suggestions for pets. As you are building your Get Away Bags from your family, make one for each pet with at least an extra leash, 3-day supply of food, treats, and a box of 1 quart plastic bags for their waste.

Checklist

Notify Immediately:
- ☐ Doctor or Coroner
- ☐ Minister & Church
- ☐ The Funeral Director
- ☐ The Cemetery or Memorial Park
  (May be handled by Funeral Home)
- ☐ Relatives & Friends
- ☐ Employer of deceased
- ☐ Musicians & Singers (Optional)
- ☐ Pallbearers (Optional)
- ☐ Insurance Agent
- ☐ Union & Fraternal Organizations
- ☐ Newspaper - Obituary
  (May be handled by Funeral Home)

Decide Immediately:
(Pre-plan if possible)
- ☐ Choice of Disposition
  (burial, cremation, organ or body donation)
- ☐ Funeral Home
- ☐ Place of Burial
- ☐ Type of Casket or Container
- ☐ Burial Clothing/Jewelry
- ☐ Flowers from Family, Casket Spray
  ### Type of Service
  - ☐ Date/Time
  - ☐ Place
  - ☐ Transportation
  - ☐ Music
  - ☐ Food before & after service

Details:
- ☐ Fill vital statistics forms for legal purposes.
- ☐ Meet with Funeral Director to plan the funeral.

- ☐ Write Obituary/Locate Obituary Photo if needed.
- ☐ Plan funeral folders with or without a photo, to pass out at the service.
- ☐ Locate friends & relatives phone numbers and addresses.
- ☐ Contact friends & relatives of deceased.
- ☐ Answer phone calls.
- ☐ Arrange lodging for out-of-town-friends & family.
- ☐ Prepare house for company before and after funeral.
- ☐ Plan for after-funeral meals.

A Reminder of Potential Expenses:
- ☐ Hospital, Doctors, & Nurses
- ☐ Ambulance/Paramedic Costs
- ☐ Coroner Transportation Costs
- ☐ Medicine
- ☐ Obituary
- ☐ Death Certificate Copies
- ☐ Purchase Cemetery Plot or Niche
- ☐ Interment
  (closing the grave, or disposing of ashes)
- ☐ Minister
- ☐ Musicians
- ☐ Florist
- ☐ Transportation
- ☐ Long Distance Telephone Calls
- ☐ Food
- ☐ Memorial marker/grave stone
- ☐ "Thank you" cards and postage

My Personal Requests

Location of Funeral or Memorial Service

Church   City   State/Province   Phone

Contact (Minister)   Address   City   State/Province   Phone

Participating Organization - Military or Fraternal

Type of Service   Open Casket   Closed Casket

Casket Style or Model   Exterior Color   Interior Color

Flag   (Yes / No)   Fold for the Family or Drape the Casket

Clothing/Jewelry/Glasses

Memorial/GravesideInstructions:

Music/Soloist _____

Favorite Scripture _____

Cemetery Information

Location of Ownership Certificate (Deed for Cemetery Property)

Cemetery   Address   City   State/Province   Phone

Preference of Burial: Lawn, Mausoleum Entombment, Cremation

_____

Memorial Marker Type (Bronze, Granite, Marble, Other)

_____

Inscription for Marker:

_____

These are my wishes   Signed   Date

Notes

The Details

Vital Statistics:

First Name   Middle Name   Last Name

Residence   City   State/Province Zip/Postal Code   Phone

Date of Birth Age   Sex State/Province & City of Birth   Race

Social Security#/Social Insurance#   Marital Status   Yrs of Education

Father's First, Middle, Last Name   Father's Birth Place

Mother's First, Middle, Last (Maiden Name)   Mother's Birth Place

Spouse's First Name   Middle Name   Last Name

Surviving Children

Other Surviving Relatives (Use additional paper to complete this information)

Military Status:

War   Branch Service #   Location of Discharge Papers

Date & Place of Entry   Date & Place of Separation

Immediate Contacts: (Additional contacts may be put on the reverse side)

#1_____

First & Last Name   Relationship

Address City   State/Province   Zip/Postal Code   Phone

#2_____

First & Last Name   Relationship

Address City   State/Province   Zip/Postal Code Phone

#3_____

First & Last Name   Relationship

Address City   State/Province   Zip/Postal Code Phone

Notes

Preferred Contacts

Funeral Director or Arrangement Counselor			Phone
Address	City	State/Province	Zip/Postal Code

Minister	Phone

Address	City	State/Province	Zip/Postal Code

Attorney	Phone

Address	City	State/Province	Zip/Postal Code

Doctor	Phone

Address	City	State/Province	Zip/Postal Code

Accountant	Phone

Address	City	State/Province	Zip/Postal Code

Personal Details:

Location of Will	Executor/Attorney	Address	Phone
Bank	Branch	Checking Acct. #	Savings Acct. #
Safe Deposit Box Location		Box Number	Location of Key
Real Estate			Location of Deed
Homeowner Insurance	Agent	Phone	Policy #	Location

Life Insurance	Agent	Phone	Policy #	Location

Car Insurance	Agent	Phone	Policy #	Location

Notes

Check it Out

It is important to understand the standard charges of local funeral homes before you need their services and how you are expected to pay for them. Duplicate this form to use as you interview funeral homes over the phone regarding their fees. This is your right, and it should be done before you need their services. If you have an immediate need, still ask for their basic service fee and embalming charges before you meet with the funeral home representative. Make sure to clarify how and when you are expected to pay for their services.

Section I—Professional Services of Funeral Home & Staff
Basic Services of the Director and Staff: $ _____
(This service may include consulting family, clergy, preparation of notices, consents, authorizations, preparing and filing death certificate prior to the funeral services.)

Additional Services & Facilities:
Visitation/Wake at funeral home for _____ hour(s) $ _____
Visitation/Wake at church or other facility for _____ hour(s) $ _____
  • Funeral or Memorial Service at funeral home
    (staff and facility) $ _____
  • Funeral or Memorial Service at church or other facility
                                                                                          $ _____
  • Graveside Service (staff) $ _____
  • Embalming Charges $ _____
  Other Preparations for the Body:
  • Casketing remains for viewing:
       Including dressing, cosmetics & hair $ _____
  • Casketing remains for closed casket:
       Dress and casket only $ _____
  • Preparing the remains when not embalming. $ _____
  • Special care for autopsied remains $ _____

Transportation: (Check on extra mileage charge outside their service area)
- Transfer remains to funeral home (from home, hospital, etc.)

  $ _____
- Funeral Car or hearse $ _____
- _____Family car(s) or limousine(s) $ _____
- Flower Car - transport flowers to service/grave $ _____
- Transfer remains to service/cemetery $ _____

Section II—Merchandice

Casket (prices range from $600 - $10,000) $ _____
Memorial Book $ _____
_____# Memorial Folders for Service $ _____
Thank You Cards _____box (es) $ _____

Section III— Non-funeral home charges incurred on your behalf.

Sales Tax $ _____
Death Certificate Copies _____# (approx. $10 - $20 each) $ _____
Permit for Disposition $ _____
Obituary $ _____
Clergy Honorarium $ _____
Organist/Soloist $ _____
Motorcycle Escort(s) $ _____
Cremation Fee $ _____
                                          TOTAL $ _____

Current funeral prices are listed at www.mylifeinabox.com/funeral.pdf

The Rest

A decision must be made concerning the resting place. Someone must decide if your loved one will be buried, or cremated. If cremation is chosen, are the ashes put in an urn and buried or dispersed in another manner? There are many options, but before the funeral can take place a decision
must be made.

Once again, here is a form. Copy it and contact local crematoriums and cemeteries to find out their costs and the availability of their services. Also be aware that you may find cemetery plots for sale in the newspaper. You may locate multiple plots that are being sold by an estate. Also keep in mind that you do not need to go through a funeral home if your loved one is going to be cremated. Many cremation services will handle all of
your needs directly through their office.

Most cemeteries have an opening and closing fee to prepare the grave. They may have an overtime charge for weekends. A vault, a liner in which the casket goes, may be required by law. The Endowment Care Fee is the charge to keep the lawn mowed around the headstone. If there is not an Endowment Care fee, the grave upkeep will belong to your family.

Cremation Only: TOTAL $ _____

A permit is required if cremains (cremation remains) are scattered in the mountains or over water.
The crematorium should have that information.

Single Burial Costs:

Grave Space	$ _____
Vault Fee	$ _____
Open & Close Grave Fee	$ _____
Endowment Care (mow lawns, etc.)	$ _____
Marker Setup Fee (to place grave stone)	$ _____
*Double Depth Burial Fee	$ _____
Pre-need Set up Fee	$ _____
TOTAL	$ _____

* Two caskets may be buried in the same grave.

Cremation Burial Costs:

In-ground Grave Space	$ _____
Above Ground Niches	$ _____
Endowment Care	$ _____
Open & Close Grave Fee	$ _____
Marker Setup Fee (to place grave stone)	$ _____
Pre-need Set up Fee	$ _____
TOTAL	$ _____

Current burial prices are listed at www.mylifeinabox.com/funeral.pdf

4 - Month Emergency Planning Calendar

Before the emergency arises, begin now and create a 7-day disaster supply kit. By using this calendar, your family can assemble an emergency kit in small steps over a period of four months.

Check off each item you collect and the actions you take each week. Get creative in how you store these items so that they are easily accessible. A large rolling plastic drum with a lid or plastic stackable tubs work well. Make sure you can lift or move them easily. Store medical supplies, flashlights and emergency items on top of other items so they can be located quickly for inspecting and restocking. Remember to rotate your perishable supplies and change water every six months. Mark your family calendar to check other supplies every three months. Talk with your family about emergency plans. Note: You should store 1–2 gallons of water per person, per day. This water is to drink and for sanitary purposes. This is why you will see the need to purchase water several times. Also in an emergency you can fill your bathtub and use your water heater as a water source. Before emptying the water heater, turn the heat source off. (Gas valve or electric plug).

WEEK ONE: *Grocery Store*

_ 1 gallon of water*
_ 1 jar of nut butter* (peanut, almond)
_ 1 jar of honey or jam
_ 1 large can of juice*
_ 1 gallon of plain liquid bleach to purify water. (8 drops per gallon)
_ Dropper measuring device (for use with bleach to treat water)
_ Hand-operated can opener
_ Instant coffee, tea, powdered drinks
_ Permanent marking pen to mark date on cans & bottled water
_ 1 gallon of water for each pet. Also: pet food, diapers, and/or baby food if needed.
_ Establish an emergency out-of-state contact.
_ Locate legal and financial documents and put them (or copies) in your My Life in a Box portable file.
_ Prepare a list of important phone numbers: out-of-state contact, physicians, veterinarian, family, creditors, insurance.
_ Pack a bag for each family member to include clothing. (See Get Away Bag plan)

_ Identify hazards you can eliminate.
_ Locate gas meter and water main shutoffs and attach the turn-off tool near each.
_ Obtain Microchip or tags for pets.

WEEK THREE: *Grocery Store*

_ 1 gallon of water*
_ 1 can of meat*
_ 1 can of fruit*
_ 1 gallon of water for each pet Also: special food for special diets.
_ Date each can of food with permanent marker.
_ Use a digital camera to photograph contents of your home for insurance purposes. Then load images on a CD or flash drive, store in Get Away Bag and send a copy to a friend or out of town family member.
_ Research your home/ rental insurance to see what it covers and if you have enough insurance. Put details on outside of policy for quick access.

WEEK TWO: *Hardware Store*

_ Crescent wrench
_ Heavy rope
_ Duct tape
_ 2 flashlights with batteries
_ 1 large box heavy duty- trash bags
_ Bungee cords in various lengths
_ Disposable lighter
_ Check your house for hazards.

*** one item per person**

WEEK FOUR: *Hardware Store*

_ 2" masking tape
_ Crow bar
_ Smoke detector with battery
_ Tarp
_ Port-a-potty or 5 gallon plastic bucket for temporary toilet.
_ Plastic bags to fit bucket.
_ Obtain extra medications or

prescription marked
"Emergency Use," if needed
_ Install or test your
  Smoke/Fire/Carbon Monoxide
  detector.
_ Replace batteries if needed.
_ Tie water heater to wall studs.

WEEK FIVE: *Grocery Store*
_ 1 gallon of water*
_ 1 can of meat*
_ 1 can of fruit*
_ 1 can of vegetables*
_ 2 rolls of toilet paper*
_ Sanitary napkins
_ Personal hygiene items: toothbrush,
  tooth paste, comb*
_ Plan emergency drills at home and
  talk about it with your children so that
  it is a normal part of your family
  conversation.

WEEK SIX: *First Aid Supplies*
Build a dedicated First Aid Kit Based on
your family needs.
_ Waterproof plastic container for first
  aid supplies
_ Pain meds, aspirin etc...
_ Small. box disposable gloves
_ Compresses.
_ Rolls of gauze, bandage, & tape.
_ Assorted adhesive bandages.
_ Cold packs
_ Sunscreen
_ Check your child's day care or school

disaster plans.
_ Purchase a camp stove, or small
  BBQ and fuel to boil water.
_ Take a first aid or CERT class.

WEEK SEVEN: *Grocery Store*
_ 1 gallon of water*
_ 1 can of ready-to-eat soup*
_ 1 can of fruit*
_ 1 can of vegetables*
_ Extra hand-operated can opener
_ 3 rolls of paper towels
_ Extra plastic baby bottles, formula
  and diapers, if needed.

WEEK EIGHT: *First Aid Supplies*
_ Scissors
_ Tweezers
_ Antiseptic cream
_ Thermometer
_ Disposable hand wipes
_ Sewing kit
_ Send favorite family and pet photos
  to family members out of state for
  safekeeping. You can also scan
  them to a CD or USB flash drive, or
  archive them on a free Internet
  source.

WEEK NINE: *Grocery Store*
_ 1 gallon of water*
_ 1 can of ready-to-eat soup*

*** one item per person**

79

_ Liquid dish soap
_ 1-gallon plain liquid bleach
_ 1 box of heavy-duty garbage bags
_ 1 box of assorted crackers
_ Assorted plastic containers with lids
_ Assorted safety pins, small
  sewing kit.
_ Dry cereal
_ Contact lens solution if needed.
_ Extra clothing like jacket, towels, hat,
  Umbrella, gloves, shoes, etc.
_ Update contents of Get Away Bag to
  comply with current weather and
  have one weekend practice using the
  contents of your bag.

WEEK TEN: *Hardware Store*
_ Waterproof portable plastic storage
  container.
_ Portable AM/FM radio (with
  batteries) or one that you crank for
  power.
_ 1 flashlight (with batteries)
_ "Child–proof" latches or other
  fasteners for your cupboards
_ Double sided tape or Velcro-type
  fasteners to secure moveable
  objects
_ Extra rope or leash for pets.
_ Space blanket, blankets or sleeping
  bag for each family member and pet.
_ Update animal vaccination records.
  Put in portable file.

WEEK ELEVEN: *First Aid Supplies*
_ Anti-diarrhea medicine
_ Rubbing alcohol
_ Activated charcoal
  (for accidental poisoning)
_ Children's vitamins
_ Purchase a non-electronic (analog)
  phone to use when power goes off.

WEEK TWELVE: *Grocery Store*
_ 1 gallon of water*
_ 1 large can of juice*
_ Large plastic food bags
_ 1 box of quick energy snacks
_ 3 rolls paper towels
_ Pen and paper for note taking.
_ Store, extra cash and credit cards
  in Get Away Bag

WEEK THIRTEEN: *Hardware Store*
_ Whistle
_ ABC Fire extinguisher
_ Pliers, Vise grips
_ Local area map
_ Hand warmers
_ Extra batteries for radio and
  flashlights
_ Camping lantern with fuel or
  batteries.
_ Large ground screw to leash animals
  to when fences fall.
_ Find out if you have a neighborhood
  Safety organization and join it!
_ Arrange for a friend or neighbor to
  watch your children or your pets if

*** one item per person**

you are at work.

_ For pets, locate appropriate size container for evacuation. Keep a small baggy of food in the pet container, with empty plastic bags for pet waste.

WEEK FOURTEEN: *Grocery Store*

_ 1 can of meat*
_ 1 can of vegetables*
_ 1 box large heavy-duty trash bags
_ 1 box quick energy snacks
_ 1 box tissues
_ Brace shelves and cabinets.
_ Secure fish tanks, bird houses and reptile cages.

WEEK FIFTEEN: *Hardware Store*

_ Extra batteries
_ Masking tape
_ Extra house & car key for Get Away Bag
_ Hammer
_ "L" brackets or flexible straps to secure tall furniture to wall studs.
_ Heavy work gloves
_ 1 box of disposable dust masks
_ Screwdriver
_ Plastic safety goggles
_ 1 box of heavy-duty garbage bags.

WEEK SIXTEEN: *Grocery Store*

_ 1 can fruit*
_ 1 can meat*
_ 1 can vegetables*
_ 1 package paper plates & ups*
_ Eating utensils
_ Adult Vitamins
_ Large plastic food bags
_ Plastic wrap & Aluminum foil
_ Make a plan to check on a neighbor who might need help in an emergency.
_ Obtain extra prescriptions and mark "For Emergency Use," if needed for family and pets. Make sure to use the original containers.

Research how you will store all of these supplies. They may be stored in a large rolling plastic drum with a watertight lid, or in stackable plastic storage tubs. Get creative and make sure the containers are easy to access.

*** one item per person**

Notes

Notes

Notes

Notes

Notes

Notes

Notes

Notes

A Special Invitation from Laurie

As a member of the *My Life in a Box Community*, I would like to offer you many of the forms in this book in an electronic format so you can update and save them easily on your computer as you experience changes in your life. For access to the PDF forms and for future updates please visit:

www.mylifeinabox.com/bookowners.html